CELEBRATING THE CITY OF HO CHI MINH CITY

Celebrating the City of Ho Chi Minh City

Walter the Educator

Silent King Books

SILENT KING BOOKS

SKB

Copyright © 2024 by Walter the Educator

All rights reserved. No part of this book may be reproduced in any manner whatsoever without written permission except in the case of brief quotations embodied in critical articles and reviews.

First Printing, 2024

Disclaimer
This book is a literary work; the story is not about specific persons, locations, situations, and/or circumstances unless mentioned in a historical context. Any resemblance to real persons, locations, situations, and/or circumstances is coincidental. This book is for entertainment and informational purposes only. The author and publisher offer this information without warranties expressed or implied. No matter the grounds, neither the author nor the publisher will be accountable for any losses, injuries, or other damages caused by the reader's use of this book. The use of this book acknowledges an understanding and acceptance of this disclaimer.

Celebrating the City of Ho Chi Minh City is a little collectible souvenir book that belongs to the Celebrating Cities Book Series by Walter the Educator. Collect them all and more books at WaltertheEducator.com

USE THE EXTRA SPACE TO TAKE NOTES AND DOCUMENT YOUR MEMORIES

HO CHI MINH CITY

In the heart where the Mekong's rivers meld,

Celebrating the City of Ho Chi Minh City

Ho Chi Minh City, tales of glory held,

A tapestry of life, old and new entwined,

Vibrant spirit, from every corner, shined.

Through bustling streets where motorbikes dance,

Past old pagodas, where histories glance,

Celebrating the City of
Ho Chi Minh City

The scent of pho and banh mi in the air,

Cultures collide, yet harmonize with flair.

Beneath neon lights, Saigon hums and breathes,

A city of dreams, where each soul weaves,

Stories of struggle, of triumph, of grace,

In every alley, a smiling face.

The Saigon River, a lifeline that flows,

Through modernity's veins, its presence bestows,

An ancient rhythm in a bustling scene,

Where past and future blend, serene.

Celebrating the City of Ho Chi Minh City

From Ben Thanh Market's clamorous stalls,

To the quietude of Jade Emperor's halls,

Echoes of the past, the French facades stand,

A colonial whisper in a dynamic land.

In parks where elders practice Tai Chi's grace,

Young lovers stroll, hand in hand, embrace,

Children's laughter rings in every street,

In Ho Chi Minh, old and new worlds meet.

Nguyen Hue's promenade, a vibrant stage,

For festivals, parades, where spirits engage,

A boulevard of dreams, where every stride,

Carries the hopes of generations, pride.

In cafes where time seems to gently pause,

Writers and thinkers reflect on the cause,

Of a nation reborn from ashes of war,

To a beacon of hope, scars no more.

Temples of worship, incense in the breeze,

Prayers whispered under banyan trees,

A city that honors both ancestors and youth,

With reverence for history and a quest for truth.

The Reunification Palace, a symbol so grand,

Of a divided past, yet a unified stand,

War remnants echo in museums' silent halls,

Celebrating the City of Ho Chi Minh City

Reminding us to break down barriers and walls.

From dawn's first light to twilight's kiss,

Ho Chi Minh City, a realm of bliss,

A place where hearts and histories bind,

In every street, a story defined.

Celebrating the City of
Ho Chi Minh City

ABOUT THE CREATOR

Walter the Educator is one of the pseudonyms for Walter Anderson. Formally educated in Chemistry, Business, and Education, he is an educator, an author, a diverse entrepreneur, and he is the son of a disabled war veteran. "Walter the Educator" shares his time between educating and creating. He holds interests and owns several creative projects that entertain, enlighten, enhance, and educate, hoping to inspire and motivate you.

Follow, find new works, and stay up to date with Walter the Educator™
at WaltertheEducator.com

www.ingramcontent.com/pod-product-compliance
Lightning Source LLC
LaVergne TN
LVHW012048070526
838201LV00082B/3857